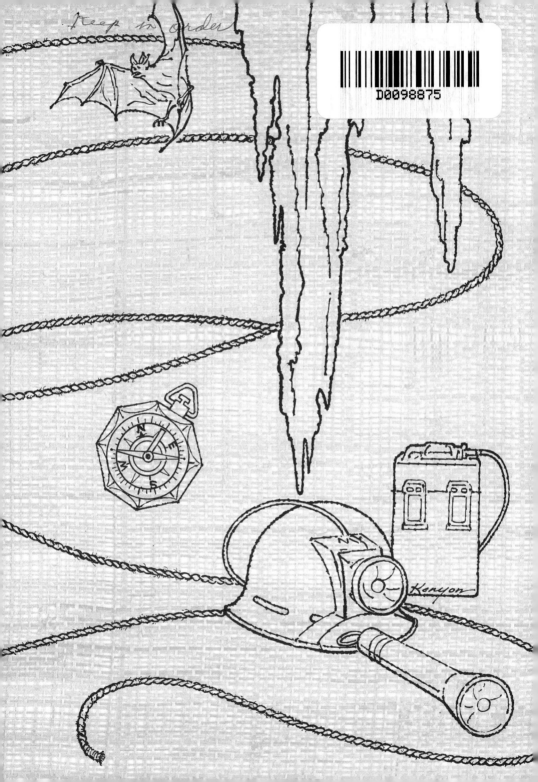

Kenyon

CAVES
and THEIR MYSTERIES

by James E. McClurg

Illustrated by
Norman Kenyon

WHITMAN PUBLISHING COMPANY
Racine, Wisconsin

Library of Congress Catalog Card Number: 62-10619

Copyright © 1962 by Whitman Publishing Company
All Rights Reserved

Printed in the U.S.A.

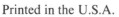

Contents

The Mystery of Caves

I'M HANGING under a waterfall. Can't you haul me up a few feet?"

"No. It's impossible."

"Then lower me back down!"

"No. We can't do that either. The winch is broken."

These were sad words to a man hanging in total darkness, suspended by a thin steel cable. Haroun Tazieff had been down in one of France's deepest caves for nine days. His friend Marcel Loubens had been killed only a few days earlier when this very cable had broken. Now Tazieff was himself in trouble almost directly over Loubens' fresh grave.

9

He could do nothing to help himself. He could not even stop his slow spinning as the cable twisted and untwisted. To make matters worse, he was hanging in the midst of a waterfall 275 feet above the cavern floor and a thousand feet below the entrance. As he became soaked with water, he was forced to drop 200,000 francs' worth of equipment to lessen the strain on the slender line that held his life in balance.

For four long hours he hung limp and exhausted in the converted parachute harness—one moment sprayed with water, the next chilled by icy blasts of air. Finally, the winch repaired, he began his slow ascent.

This man was a *speleologist,* a cave scientist, ready to risk his life for adventure and science.

Since the beginning of time, caves have been places of mystery. The ancients used them for secret religious rituals and for tombs. Some of our western Indians believed that their ancestors

rose out of great holes in the ground. Our American folklore is full of tales about the cave adventures of animals, Indians, pirates, and slaves. Let's see why people find caves so interesting.

We humans are curious creatures. We have found out a great deal about the bottom of the deepest ocean and about the top of the highest mountain. We even know quite a lot about space. But we know very little about caves. We have not even completely explored such famous caves as the Carlsbad Caverns in New Mexico or Mammoth Cave in Kentucky. Because so little is known about caves, thousands of amateur explorers go into them each year. These explorers, called *spelunkers,* hope to set foot where no one has ever been before.

A second group of spelunkers explore caves because of the challenge they offer. A great deal of skill, strength, and nerve is needed to explore caves like Neff's Canyon Cave in Utah. Spelunking in this cave has been described as

Neff's Canyon Cave, Utah, has so many cliffs and canyons that only the most experienced cavers are allowed into its dangerous depths.

11

"mountain climbing at night."

There is still another group of explorers. These men are happiest when they find a cave in which people lived long, long years ago. Called *archeologists*, these scientists have discovered that some caves can be read almost like history books. Instead of turning pages, they simply peel back the layers of dirt and rubble on the floor. The things they find at each level tell them what kind of human beings lived there and something about the animals that lived at the same time. The deeper these scientists go, the older are the remains they find. Almost all we know about prehistoric man has come from caves.

It is interesting that almost all of us have the same mental picture of caves. Closing our eyes, we think of: long narrow passageways leading in circles; total darkness; bats; huge rooms with strange objects hanging from the ceiling; water dripping down to put out the weak, flickering candle that is our only light; and dead silence.

More than 40 tons of fossilized bones have been taken from the Port Kennedy Bone Cave in Pennsylvania.

Crust

Mantle

Molten Core

At the Earth's core the temperature is estimated to be 9000° F. The pressure is estimated to be 54 trillion pounds per square inch.

A Cave Is Not Always a Cave

BOY, AM I GLAD to get back to solid ground!" Think how many times you have heard this remark. However, even a little knowledge of geology—the science that deals with the study of the Earth—would reveal that the ground is not nearly as solid as we once imagined.

If we could take a trip from the center of the Earth outward to the surface, our first 2,200 miles would be through part of the Earth's semiliquid *core*. This core is thought to be made of nickel and iron under very high temperature and pressure.

Mountains are formed by movement of the Earth's crust.

The next 1,800 miles would carry us through a layer of rock called the *mantle*. No human being has ever seen a piece of the mantle. But it is believed to be a dark, heavy, coarse rock known only as *ultrabasic* by the geologists.

The final and shortest part of our trip would be through the *crust* and into open air. This crust forms a very thin layer on the outside of the Earth much like the skin on an apple. The Earth's crust varies from five to forty miles in thickness. This layer is very important because it is here that we find all the oil wells, mineral deposits, mountains, valleys, and caves.

The Earth's crust is constantly and slowly forming "wrinkles" which we call mountains. As the wrinkles form so do small cracks and open spaces. In fact, we can say that there is no such thing as a perfectly solid rock. They all have cracks and open spaces in them. Most of these cracks and spaces are so small they can be seen only with a microscope, and even then some are too small to be visible. And yet these minute cracks and spaces are very important, as we shall see. For they allow water to work its way down into the crust. The action of the water slowly wears away the rock. Every now and then a rock develops spaces or cracks that are actually big enough to crawl into. These large openings we call caves.

Although most people think that caves are rare, there are actually over five thousand known, named caves in the United States. It has been estimated that over forty thousand are awaiting discovery.

There are many different kinds of caves. Each has a special name which usually tells us either how the cave was formed or the type of rock in which it is found. Scientists call any cave that is in limestone a *cavern*. Because almost all caves are in limestone, we probably should be using the word *cavern* more often than the word *cave*.

15

However, it doesn't seem to matter which word we use unless we are talking to a geologist or speleologist.

Let's take a look at a few types of caves. As the American pioneers rode through the West and Southwest, they came upon many old volcanoes. They often looked very carefully for caves around these volcanoes, for lava caves often contain ice the year around.

These *lava caves* or *lava tubes* are not very big. Generally they measure less than a few hundred feet long, although some may be almost a mile in length. Some are the result of a large amount of gas having bubbled up through the hot, liquid lava. However, most lava tubes were formed when the surface lava cooled and hardened while the inside continued to flow. Soon all that was left was a thin roof over long winding open spaces. The best lava caves are found in Hawaii and Iceland.

Lava Beds National Monument, California, has 297 explored lava caves.

The Indians of the Southwest lived for many centuries in shallow caves that had been hollowed out of the cliffs by wind and blowing sand. Most of these *wind caves* are not true caves. They are just open spaces beneath overhanging ledges.

The name *wind cave* may also be given to a limestone cavern that has a large amount of air blowing in or out of it. Wind Cave, South Dakota, is an example of this type. It was discovered by a pioneer named Tom Bingham who stopped to rest one day and heard the sound of rushing air. He soon found a small hole that had so much air blowing out that it held his hat suspended above the ground. The next day he took some friends out to show them this strange hole. Carefully he pushed his hat over it. With a loud *slurp* the hat disappeared into the ground forever! That day the cave happened to be "breathing" in.

Along many a coastline

waves pounding against a cliff have slowly eroded away the rock, resulting in a *sea cave*. Some sea caves can be entered only by boat, some only during low tide. Skin divers have recently discovered many new sea caves whose entrances could not be seen from the surface.

Most caves and caverns are made by water, and water is found almost everywhere. But one of the places where you would not expect to find it is deep inside a glacier. Surprisingly, there are actually small rivers flowing deep within most glaciers. This water comes from melting ice at the surface and works its way down through cracks and crevices. In places the rivers have melted enough ice to form good-sized caves. Many of these *ice caves* have

Fingal's Cave, in the Hebrides Islands off the coast of Scotland, was once the hiding place of pirates.

Exploring an ice cave deep inside a glacier is a dangerous task.

become popular tourist attractions and even places of worship. Thousands of Hindus make pilgrimages high into the Himalayan Mountains each year to view the sacred ice in the ice cave of Amaranth.

The term *ice cave* is sometimes used for any cave that has ice in it. So-called ice caves in the United States are merely ice-filled lava caves or caverns, not true ice caves.

Poets and writers often speak of "mysterious grottoes." They use the word *grotto* as a fancy word for cave. To a spelunker a grotto is a large room within a cave.

In addition to the caves we have already mentioned, spelunkers speak of *live* and *dead* caves. A live cave is one that is getting bigger; water is continually entering and leaving. A dead cave is simply one that is not growing larger. It is dry and the many beautiful formations are beginning to crumble to dust. Most caves are a combination of the two—parts are live and parts are dead.

19

A Visit to a Cave Factory

GEOLOGISTS ARE very much like detectives. They search through the rocks of the world for clues. These clues help them figure out what our Earth looked like hundreds, millions, even billions of years ago. One of the more unusual facts geologists have discovered is that every part of America was covered by an ocean at some time in the long-ago past. These broad, shallow oceans often remained for millions of years.

In many places the ocean bottoms were slowly covered with a thick layer of limy mud and animal shells. Thousands of feet of this ooze were often deposited. In the years to follow, this material was squeezed and hard-

Shells and minerals settle to the sea floor. Under great pressure, in time this layer turns into limestone.

ened into a rock called lime-stone. After a time pressures within the crust of the Earth slowly raised the ocean bottoms. The seas drained away. At last all the rock lay exposed for the first time to wind, rain, and sunlight. Be-

Mountains are often made of limestone.

cause of these oceans, many parts of the United States have layers of limestone just beneath the soil.

People who know very little about geology or chemistry are often puzzled as to why most caves occur in limestone. Limestone is not a soft, crumbly rock as many people believe. It is actually quite hard—hard enough to be used as a building stone. And this is the puzzler. In one breath the scientist says limestone is tough enough to make a good building stone. In the next breath he says

Shell forms can be seen in limestone.

that almost all caves are found in limestone because it is so easily eroded away.

The secret lies in soda pop. The gas that causes the fizz and bubbles in pop is carbon dioxide. You may have seen the abbreviation for carbon dioxide: CO_2. Carbon dioxide dissolves very easily in water, forming weak carbonic acid. Pure water can wash over limestone for a long time with very little effect. But if the water contains any acid the rock will dissolve quite easily.

Although carbonic acid is very weak it is still strong enough to eat away the limestone. You can see how this works by putting a little vinegar—a weak acid—on a piece of chalk, which is made of the same material as limestone. Watch the little bubbles that form as the acid dissolves the chalk.

But—how does carbon dioxide get into water? Although most people think so, rain is not pure water. Each drop of rain contains a tiny speck of dust, and as the rain falls through the air it picks up carbon dioxide from the atmosphere. More carbon dioxide is added as the water

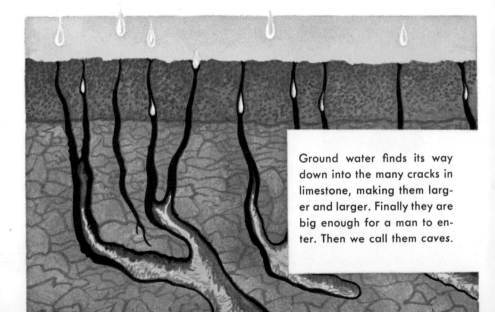

Ground water finds its way down into the many cracks in limestone, making them larger and larger. Finally they are big enough for a man to enter. Then we call them caves.

Lost River in southern Indiana one day suddenly disappeared into a sinkhole in its path. It reappeared seven miles farther on.

seeps through the first few feet of soil. By the time the water reaches limestone there is always a small amount of acid present. However, do not get the idea that this water will go through limestone like warm water through ice. It still takes thousands of years to form a cave big enough to walk into.

Caves frequently form so close to the surface that the roof finally collapses. From the surface, these cave-ins look like big round holes in the ground. Geologists call them *sinks* or *sinkholes*. A few may extend one hundred feet across and reach a depth of one hundred feet. Sinkholes are almost sure clues that caves may be found nearby. In some places in southern Indiana there are as many as one thousand sinkholes in a square mile.

As time goes on, the caves grow larger. The cracks become connected, and the ground water collects in underground pools and rivers. Some of these rivers run for miles and miles before they pour out through a cave entrance and join a regular river. In many cave areas almost all the creeks and rivers are underground.

As you see, every cave must have at least two openings: one for the water to get in and one for it to get out. Usually, though, the water enters through thousands of small cracks and leaves through one big opening.

Ninety per cent of all caves—and all of the really large caves in the world, such as Mammoth Cave and Carlsbad Caverns—were formed in the way we have just described.

The river emerging at Silver Springs, Florida, brings up 600 tons of dissolved minerals a day.

Moon Milk and Soda Straws

A WIDE-AWAKE TRIP to fairyland." That is the best way to describe a person's first trip into one of the many well-decorated caves like Luray Caverns in West Virginia or Wyandotte Cave in Indiana. Caves are a little like birthday cakes. Some have very little decoration while others are a wonderland of fancy frills and trimmings.

How do the decorations get inside a cave? Nature has a special recipe for cave frosting. It calls for water, minerals, and last but not least, plenty of time.

Ground water seeps down from the surface and coats

ceilings, walls, and floors of all live caves. As the water moves through the walls and roof of the cave it slowly dissolves away part of the limestone. Limestone is a rock made up almost entirely of one mineral, calcite. It is the calcite that the water dissolves. The other minerals, such as clay, are usually simply washed away.

Almost all of the minerals dissolved by ground water finally find their way out of the cave. Fortunately for us the cave rivers are not really greedy; they leave a little calcite behind each year. Over a period of thousands of years this "left behind and forgotten" calcite forms our cave frosting.

Let's see how minerals are left behind before we take a look at the different types of *speleothems*—that's the scientific word for cave decorations. If we had eyes powerful enough to look inside a drop of water collecting on the ceiling of a cave, we would find it completely filled with dissolved minerals—so full that it could not possibly hold any more. Geologists would say that the drop was "saturated" with minerals.

The drop usually clings to the ceiling for a few seconds

before falling. This is just long enough for a little of the water to evaporate. Curiously enough, only the water evaporates and not the minerals. The drop, smaller in size, cannot hold as much dissolved mineral matter as it did before some of the water evaporated. So as the drop falls microscopic bits of calcite remain sticking to the ceiling. If drops continue to form at the same spot for years and years, a small bump will appear. Gradually this bump will grow bigger and perhaps take the shape of an icicle. Speleologists call such icicles *stalactites*. *Stalactite* comes from a Greek word meaning "oozing out of drops." For some reason stalactites, especially small ones, often have a small hole through the center.

But getting back to our drop of water, a little more will evaporate from this same drop when it falls from the ceiling to the floor of the cave. Again, specks of calcite will begin collecting. They will build an upside-down icicle

Greatly enlarged, a drop of water would be found to be packed with dissolved minerals.

Stalactites 40 feet long and 10 feet thick have been found in Luray Caverns, West Virginia.

Stalactites

Stalagmites

known as a *stalagmite*. Stalagmites—from a Greek word meaning "a dripping" —are usually thicker and more rounded than the long, pointed stalactites. You can remember the two words, stalactite and stalagmite, by saying "Stalac*tites* stick *tightly* to the ceiling and stalag*mites might* get up there if they work hard enough." Many times two grow together, forming a column.

However, a stalagmite is not always found directly beneath a stalactite. Possibly the water dripped too fast to form a stalagmite. Or the drops may have fallen off the stalactite into a pool of water so that no stalagmite was formed.

One rare type of stalactite looks like a long pencil with a hole through the center. These curious little tubes are called *soda straws*. Soda straws three and one half feet long were found in Boone's Mill Cave, Indiana.

Cave decorations formed by drops of falling water are called *dripstones*. Those that are formed when water

Flowstones

Dripstones

Rimstones

Calcite Balls

Stalagmites 62 feet high and 20 feet thick have been found in Carlsbad Caverns, New Mexico.

flows evenly along a wall or crack are called *flowstones*. Flowstones often take shapes resembling curtains, veils, or drapes. Some of these ring like church bells when struck with a hammer.

As the water in cave pools evaporates, a band of calcite forms around the edges. This *rimstone* acts as a natural dam causing the water level to rise. One may sometimes see cave pearls clustered on the bottom. The calcite forms around some small object in just the same way that a real pearl forms within an oyster.

The objects spelunkers treasure most—and the hardest to find—are small, fragile calcite balls that have enough air trapped inside so that they will float about in the cave pools.

The most peculiar oddities found within a cave are small slender stalactites that seem to have lost their respect for gravity. These curious little fellows twist and curl in all directions—including straight up. Scientists still puzzle about how these *helictites* form. They are quite common in mines as well as in caves.

Although most cave decorations are white or gray, many have been tinted cream, orange, red, or even blue by small amounts of impurities such as iron. A ribbon-like flowstone may have a few layers of white calcite followed by bands of red calcite making it look like bacon.

It is not possible to say exactly how fast a speleothem will grow. It depends upon many things such as the amount of water present, the amount of calcite in the water, and the humidity inside the cave. One stalactite is known to have increased one inch in diameter in one hundred years. Another grew

Moon Milk

twelve inches longer in only ten years.

Soft pasty-looking *moon milk* is a special kind of stalagmite which, it is believed, contains so much water that it cannot solidify completely. It is found in caverns where evaporation cannot take place because the air is already saturated with moisture.

Although the various kinds of dripstone and flowstone make up most of the cave frosting, there is much more for the spelunker to see. Often he may come upon huge blocks of rubble or *breakdown*. It looks as though most of the ceiling had fallen in. A glance up is all that is needed to convince him that it really did, for he may

Helictites

Calcite Balls

Breakdown

find himself looking up at a high domelike roof a hundred feet over his head.

Not only must the spelunker crawl over large piles of breakdown, but in many caves the floor he is walking on will simply disappear. A great gaping hole will drop away at his feet. His feeble light will not reach to the bottom of that hole.

Not all parts of a cave are like the big tunnels and rooms we have been describing. Some places are very narrow indeed. In order to enter the largest part of Floyd Collins' Crystal Cave the eager spelunker must wriggle on his stomach for 1,300 feet. The ceiling gets lower and lower until at one point the opening is only ten inches high!

One last thing in caves is especially noticeable. But it's something you don't really discover until after you are outside once more. You look down, and you find yourself saying, "There sure must be a lot of mud in that cave. Just look at my boots!"

A spelunker must be prepared to crawl through tiny spaces.

Spelunking

A FLICKERING yellowish glow eased its way cautiously across the cavern and came to rest on a mud-caked man sitting on a large block of breakdown.

"Bill," a cheery voice echoed toward the seated man, "you look like a mountain climber, gold miner, and scrub woman all rolled into one large mud ball."

"You wouldn't win any awards in the Easter parade yourself in that outfit," Bill laughingly replied.

And of course both men were perfectly correct. For the spelunker's uniform is designed for use and comfort, not for looks. On their heads the men wore narrow-brimmed hard hats similar to those worn by miners and construction workers. The hard hat is a most valuable piece of equipment, for even a small rock can be deadly if it falls very far. In addition, the hat prevents water from dripping into the spelunker's eyes and also provides a place to clip his carbide lamp. Small, efficient, fist-sized, the carbide lamp uses only water and a chemical called calcium carbide. The water drips into the carbide and produces acetylene gas which burns with a bright yellow flame. One filling lasts several hours.

Each man wore one-piece coveralls that had a leather patch around the upper part of one leg and another over the opposite shoulder. The coveralls keep the caver warm, fairly dry, and mud free. The leather patches protect his leg and shoulder from rope burns as he lowers himself down cliffs.

Thick rubber pads were strapped about the men's knees for protection and comfort as they crawled or wriggled through narrow passages.

Fancy shoes have no place in caves, so each man wore heavy work shoes or hiking boots. Wet feet are bad enough; but *cold,* wet feet can make the most exciting cave seem miserable.

Turning a caver upside down and shaking him would reveal a whole pile of odds and ends that had been stuffed into pockets or hung on belts. As all spelunkers should carry three types of light, we would expect to find matches, candles, flashlight, a small can of carbide, and sometimes a canteen of water. A watch and compass would be found somewhere in the pile because it is very easy to lose one's sense of time and direction underground. And we might find one of the newest items to be used by cavers: a thirty-foot collapsible ladder. This amazing little ladder is made of steel cables and aluminum alloy rungs and weighs only two pounds.

Deep inside the pile we would probably find a first aid kit, a repair kit for the carbide lamps, a roll of plastic reflecting tape to be used in marking the trail, a whistle, a pocket knife, and probably a squashed sandwich. But no

35

ball of string! It would take a huge amount of string to allow a person to explore very far into a cave. Can you imagine carrying five miles of string? Instead, spelunkers carefully place markers here and there to keep track of the way out. Rocks may be piled on the floor, or arrows scratched on the walls. Other marks may also be made with chalk or tape, or by holding the carbide lamp close to the wall, causing a smudge. No matter what kind of markers are used, all point toward the entrance.

One of the most recent gadgets to be used inside a cave is the Aqualung. These and other SCUBA units are used by trained divers to examine underground rivers that

Underwater cave chambers, never before entered, are now being explored using diving equipment.

may be the only way into a vast network of unexplored chambers.

Just having the correct equipment does not make it safe to enter a cave. Spelunkers also have important safety rules which should always be followed. These rules as well as most of the equipment described earlier apply only to "wild" caves and not to the electrically lighted commercial caves open to tourists.

In spite of all safety precautions, strange accidents have occurred in caves. A man in Texas decided to start a fire in a cave full of bat guano, droppings. Unfortunately he discovered too late that aging guano contains a large amount of potassium nitrate which is a very powerful explosive.

Although without water we would have no caverns, it is also water that presents one of the gravest dangers to spelunkers. Cavers should pay close attention to the outside weather because a sudden heavy rain could cause a flash flood in one of the lower chambers. Just a few years ago six out of eight speleologists were trapped and drowned in a flash flood while studying cave insects in a very deep cave in France.

37

Another danger often present is that of polluted water. Because all water in a cave originally came from the surface, it could easily have flowed through a barnyard before it reached the cave. As a matter of fact, some farmers have used sinkholes as a convenient place to dump dead animals. Cities, too, have used them for garbage pits and cesspools. Although cave water is often safe to drink it is not wise to do so unless it has been tested.

Unlike the water, air in a cave is almost always safe. Only a very few caves contain any poisonous gases. Kiser Cave near Mason, Texas, is an exception because it con-

Safety Rules for All Cavers

Always have an adult with you.

Never go into a cave alone. It is safest to go in groups of three. If someone is injured, one person can give first aid while another goes for help.

Always tell someone where and when you are going and when you plan to return. In case you are all trapped, help will be sent when you do not appear at the correct time.

Always carry at least three different sources of light: a carbide lamp or electric head lamp for general use, a flashlight for use when a strong beam of light is needed, and finally a thick candle in case of emergency.

Always wear a hard hat. They have prevented a lot of headaches.

tains almost pure carbon dioxide. The source of the carbon dioxide is not known. But we do know that some oil wells in Texas have also hit pockets of the pure gas. Three spelunkers daringly entered parts of Kiser cave using Air Force oxygen masks.

An organization called the National Speleological Society, Inc. (NSS) has been set up to aid amateurs in all phases of spelunking. The society publishes articles on caving, holds training classes, and conducts trips. Hundreds of cave maps are on sale at the national office in Washington, D.C. The society has over forty branches, called grottoes, scattered throughout the country.

Never go beyond your experience. For example, if you have never climbed cliffs, used ropes, or climbed to great heights on a ladder, do not do these things for the first time in a cave. Practice on safer ground first.

Remember These Rules, Too

Many caves are on private land. Get permission from the owner to go exploring.

Leave the cave as you found it. Explorers who follow you should not be forced to look at broken stalactites or signs reading "John loves Mary."

Home
Sweet
Home

A CAVE is very much like a deserted hotel. A quick glance would lead us to conclude that no one lives there. However, if we searched the hotel carefully, prying under boards and looking into dark corners, we would find many small animals and perhaps some big ones. The same careful search must be used in a cave. Most people who go into a cave never see a single animal. However, zoologists—scientists who study animals—and botanists —scientists who study plants—tell us that over a hundred kinds of animals and a very few plants live in caves.

Most plants make their own food. To do this, they need sunlight and a green substance called chlorophyll.

Mushrooms and molds do not make their own food, so these nongreen plants are able to survive in complete darkness. Before we talk about cave animals, let's play detective. Let's see if we can figure out what a cave animal should look like. We know that caves are dark, damp, and that the temperature in them seldom changes. We also know that there is very little food inside them. Using these facts, we can imagine what a cave animal might look like.

Because it is dark, he would need no eyes. If none of the animals could see, there would be no need for protective coloring, so he might as well be colorless. If an animal cannot see to find food, he would have to have a good sense of hearing, touch, and taste. Because large animals eat large quantities of food every day, we would expect cave animals to be quite small. And finally, since the temperature inside caves does not change, he would need no heavy coat of fur for protection against rapid changes in temperature.

41

A pawprint was their first clue that a jaguar had entered the cave.

Explorers of Craighead Caverns, Tennessee, found the bones of a jaguar.

Now we do not expect all cave animals to look as we have just imagined them. But let's keep these characteristics in mind as we examine a few.

Just like the visitors to our imaginary hotel, cave animals can be divided into four groups: occasional visitors, part-time roomers, a few uninvited guests who drop in, and the permanent residents.

Almost every kind of animal known to man from a lion to a mosquito has been a visitor to a cave at some time. These visitors usually do not go into the dark regions and they seldom remain long. Scientists recently discovered a big paw print deep in Craighead Caverns in eastern Tennessee. A cast was made and compared to the paws of large animals in a New York zoo. The track was undoubtedly made by a jaguar. But jaguars were never known to have inhabited the United States. Further exploration revealed the bones of this big cat that had

Pack rats and bats are part-time roomers in caves. Eight million bats spend their days in Carlsbad Caverns. It takes them four hours to leave at dusk, and four more hours to return at dawn.

apparently wandered too far into the cave and died of starvation. On this new evidence, scientists now believe that jaguars at one time roamed at least as far north as Tennessee.

The part-time roomers divide their time between the cave and the outside world, going out to find food or a mate. Pack rats and bats are two of the most common part-time roomers.

Most people are surprised to learn that bats are not birds at all. They belong to the class of animals called mammals. Mammals have fur or hair, and give birth to live babies rather than laying eggs. They have a skeleton on the inside, rather than on the outside like beetles and lobsters. And they feed their babies on mother's milk. Bats are the only mammals that fly. Flying squirrels are mammals, but they really just glide. Bats are helpful to man because they live on insects. Only a few varieties in

A bat sends out a high-pitched sound too high for the human ear to hear. The sound bounces off objects in front of the bat, returning to him so that he can steer clear of them.

Central America and Mexico carry disease or drink blood.

Bats have very small, weak eyes and big ears. They depend on a type of radar called echo-location to guide them through the dark. Their radar is so good they can dodge wires hanging in front of them.

Many animals whose remains have been found in caves did not go in on purpose. Most of these uninvited guests fell down sinkholes or vertical entrances and could not get out. Almost all the common animals have appeared as uninvited guests.

Let's meet the permanent residents. These are the true cave animals. Many people think that true cave animals are trapped in caves. This is not true. They are there because they find it easy to live in caves. In fact, most cave animals at some time in the past willingly moved into caves because they did not like the outside world!

Blindfish are the most famous of the permanent residents. They are very small. A full-grown *Amblyopsis spelaeus* from Mammoth Cave is just three inches long. Not only are some of the cave fish blind, but in many varieties one cannot even see any sign of an eye or eye socket. Some are so transparent that they were discovered only when a speleologist saw shadows of fish moving along the bottom of a pool! Although there are about twenty-five varieties of true cave fish, none of them produce their own light as do some fish that live in the dark ocean depths.

The best known blindfish is the *Amblyopsis spelaeus* found in Mammoth Cave.

Beetle

Salamander

An alert speleologist can
find blind salamanders, crayfish, crickets, spiders, beetles,
ants, and flatworms. Most of these
are colorless, but many still do things
that their relatives of the outside world
do even though the effort may seem useless
in a cave. Some spiders, for example, spin webs
and cocoons. One species of cricket cannot chirp
but has feelers or antennae seven times as long as his body.

Interestingly enough, no bird or reptile has ever become a true cave dweller. These animals do not seem to
be able to adapt to cave life.

Cave supermarkets do not exist. Cave animals find that
food is very scarce. In fact, all food must come from the
outside. It may be carried in by the wind, or by the part-
time roomers. But most of the minerals and pieces of
organic material needed as food are dissolved in water
and seep into the cave from the Earth's surface.

46

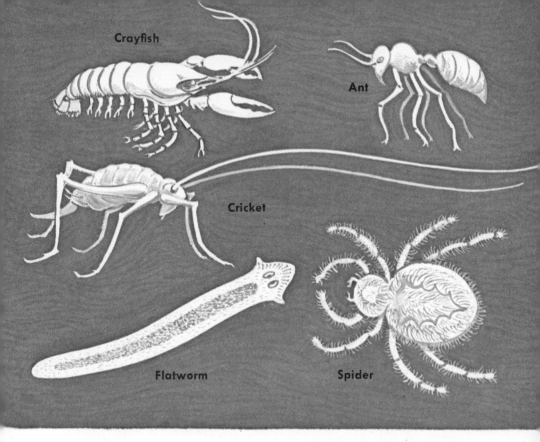

Crayfish

Ant

Cricket

Flatworm

Spider

Scientists still puzzle over the question of whether cave animals were blind before they entered caves or became so afterward. At first it seemed reasonable to believe that if a fish never used its eyes, it would soon become blind. This may be true. Nevertheless, babies of this fish would still be born with good eyes; but babies of cave fish do not have eyes. Zoologists now tend to agree that most cave animals have changed little since they entered caves.

All in all, our curious little cave animals are happy and content in their cave hotel.

Mushrooms, Moneybags, and Mines

CAVES ARE JUST HOLES in the ground, but people have thought up amazing things to do with them.

Early man discovered that caves made fine homes. They were cool in the summer and warm in the winter. So many of these people moved into caves that when we think of prehistoric humans we usually speak of *cave men*. Even today, many people in France, Tunisia, and China prefer to live underground. In fact, the whole French village of Roche L'Eveque in the valley of the Loire River is a *troglodyte* town. People whose homes are in caves are called troglodytes.

Caves made comfortable homes for early man.

The village of Haute-Isle, France, is a troglodyte town. Most of its buildings are underground.

Caves have long been used as hiding places for both people and valuable goods. Jesse James might be considered one of the early spelunkers, for he is supposed to have hidden $100,000 in gold coins in a cave in Missouri. Counterfeiters at one time used Cave-in-Rock on the banks of the Ohio River in southern Illinois. This was a busy cave, for shortly after the counterfeiters moved out a band of river pirates moved in.

In 1884, a group of four men robbed a Union Pacific train of $62,000 near Tucson, Arizona. The sheriff trailed them to the entrance of Colossal Cave and decided to camp there until they came out. A few days later, he received word that the thieves had discovered another opening. They were in the nearby town laughing about fooling the sheriff. Although they were quickly caught, the money was never found. The empty Wells Fargo moneybags were discovered in the cave many years later by spelunkers.

Caves have even served as a type of railroad station. Before and during the Civil War, many slaves escaped and made their way north on what was called the Underground Railroad. It really was not a railroad, but simply a series of secret routes and hiding places. Many caves including such famous ones as Mammoth Cave and Meramec Caverns served as secret "stations" or daylight hiding places. One such cave on the banks of the Delaware

Caves along the route of the Underground Railroad sheltered slaves during the Civil War.

Caves have even been used as prisons.

River had a secret escape route through a trap door in the floor of a farmer's house. The recent owners finally had to seal off the escape route because spelunkers kept appearing in their living room!

So far these uses are just what you might expect. But hold on, because we have just started. It seems that humans have used caves for everything except airports and sunbathing!

Marvel Cave in Missouri and Newgate Cave in Connecticut were both used as prisons. Newgate Prison is open to the public. Visitors may enter its dark, damp chambers to see the manacles and chains that were used to hold prisoners during the Revolutionary War.

On the brighter side of things, a number of caves have a room called the bridal chamber where cave operators actually allow weddings to be performed. Bridal Cave in Missouri often holds a number of weddings each week.

51

Cave weather prediction: little change in temperature, cool, damp, light winds in some areas; excellent for mushroom beds.

Back in 1850, a cave played an important part in the first air-conditioned hotel. A few miles east of Cobleskill, New York, a farmer named Lester Howe built a hotel to house visitors to his then newly discovered and now famous cave, Howe Caverns. To make eating more pleasant he piped cool cave air into the dining room.

Farmers near Frepillon, France, found that nearby caves were excellent places to grow mushrooms. They hauled soil and fertilizer into the cool damp caves and set up huge underground mushroom farms. Some caves contain as many as twenty-six miles of mushroom beds producing three thousand pounds of mushrooms a day.

Spelunkers of the future should beware of at least one cave. The Bethlehem Steel Company converted one of the Reddington caves near Bethlehem, Pennsylvania, into a firing range for testing artillery shells. And shells do not always go off when they are supposed to!

Probably the oldest profitable cave activity is the mining of nitrates, or saltpeter as it is often called. These chemicals are usually found either mixed with dirt on the cave floor or as part of bat droppings. They are used in the manufacture of explosives and fertilizers. Most of the gunpowder used in the War of 1812 and the Civil War was made from nitrates mined from many United States caves. An underground chemical plant run by slaves was set up in Mammoth Cave about 1812. Pipes made of hollow logs were used to carry water down to the mixing vats.

Just a few years ago someone found a small cave filled with bat guano deep within the Grand Canyon. A cable-car down to the cave was built to remove the material.

In addition, caves have been used as cold storage rooms for food, as chicken farms, as a railroad tunnel (Southern Railway in southwest Virginia), water reservoirs, cheese-aging rooms, "moonshine" stills, and dance halls. All in all, though, the best thing to do with a cave is to make it a tourist attraction.

The cool dampness of caves is also excellent for aging cheese.

How to Find a Cave

WELL OVER FOUR THOUSAND United States caves are listed in the files of the National Speleological Society. Most—but not all—were found simply by accident or pure luck.

Lester Howe wondered why all his cows stood in a particular part of the field every time the weather was hot. He wandered over to them and felt a cool breeze blowing from under a large rock. He rolled the rock away and discovered what is now the famous Howe Caverns, near Cobleskill, New York.

A hunter is supposed to have discovered Mammoth Cave after chasing a wounded bear into the entrance.

Jim White thought he saw smoke rising in the foothills. That dark column turned out to be not smoke, but hundreds of thousands of bats. The hole from which they flew was the entrance to Carlsbad Caverns.

And cowboy Jim White discovered Carlsbad Caverns after watching the bats fly out of it. Almost every cave has some story like this connected with its discovery.

On the other hand, Skyline Caverns in West Virginia was found by a geologist after a careful scientific search. Walter Amos knew that most caves were formed in limestone and that there were large amounts of limestone close to the surface in a particular spot in the state. He studied the geology of the area to discover which way the ground water moved and picked the most likely area for a cave. He then found a valley at this location where the limestone was exposed on a cliff face. And finally he found the cavern that he "just knew" had to be there.

The best guess at the moment is that there are about

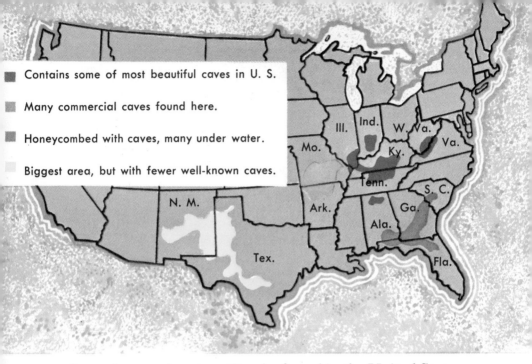

Contains some of most beautiful caves in U. S.

Many commercial caves found here.

Honeycombed with caves, many under water.

Biggest area, but with fewer well-known caves.

forty thousand caves still to be found in the United States. Certainly not all of them could be found by purely scientific means. But the chances are better if you at least have some idea of where to look. Limestone can be found in nearly every state. However, there are four major cavern regions as shown on the map on this page.

To aid in our search it would help if we knew where caves are not found. The Rocky Mountains and most of the New England states are made of granite and other igneous rocks. These rocks are so tough that only very rarely will a cave be found in them, and even then it will probably be very small.

The North Central states—North Dakota, South Dakota, most of Montana, Nebraska, Minnesota, Wisconsin, and Michigan—make up an almost caveless area. It is not because of a lack of limestone here, for there are large limestone beds under most of these states. The problem is that these states were covered by four different glaciers, the last one melting away just eight thousand years ago. This is practically yesterday to a geologist who thinks of a million years as a short time. Each glacier left a layer of sand, gravel, and clay spread fairly evenly over the entire area. This glacial debris or *till* is usually a few hundred feet thick and is over a thousand feet thick in some places.

However, there is a spot near Alpena, Michigan, where the glacial till is less than ten feet thick. Many sinkholes and cracks have been found there. This area presents an exciting challenge to future spelunkers.

How do you find a cave entrance? This is more difficult than simply locating cave regions. Since most big entrances have already been found, you will have to put your eyes to the ground and look for small clues. Look

under bushes and at the bases of trees. The bare rock is more often exposed in these places. Small, cool drafts of air have been giveaways to large caves. Steep valley walls and new road cuts are particularly good hunting grounds. Animal trails and springs may also lead to caves. And sinkholes and disappearing streams are, of course, dead giveaways.

One last word before you pack up to go spelunking. You may be fortunate enough to discover something really valuable, such as a human skeleton or animal bones. Do not disturb them. Trained scientists can learn a lot by studying the position of the pieces. Instead, write or go to the local university, State Geological Survey, or to the National Speleological Society and describe your find. Who knows! You may have discovered an animal that scientists believed never lived in the United States.

Good luck, Spelunker!

It's Fun to Know

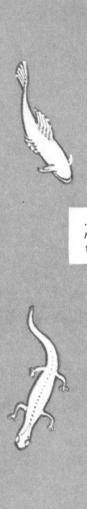

. . . that Mexican free-tailed bats fly out of Carlsbad Caverns in a counterclockwise spiral. They fly straight out of any other cave.

. . . that Devil's Hole Cave 70 miles west of Las Vegas, Nevada, contains a 90° F. spring.

. . . that the cave town of Haute-Isle, France, has an underground church. Only the steeple is visible aboveground.

. . . that Mammoth Cave contains 75 kinds of blind animals.

. . . that Carlsbad Caverns is one of the world's largest caves. One of its rooms is more than a mile long, with a ceiling 250 feet above the floor.

What is a "GISMO"?

Who eats "woodburgers"?

Can you bounce a Ping-pong ball on water?

You'll learn about these interesting things in the

Whitman Learn About Books

Have you often wondered about the trees, flowers, and animals that you see in the park or forest? And wouldn't you like to learn about how planes fly, and why a big building goes way down before it goes up? You'll find out about these things, and many others, in the Whitman Learn About Books listed below.

1. THE AIRPORT, OUR LINK TO THE SKY
Tells about radar, instrument landings, strange cargoes, what airport crews, weathermen, and flight crews do.

2. ANIMALS OF THE FIELD AND FOREST
Tells about small animals—skunks, woodchucks, opossums—and big ones—bears, deer, and moose. These and many more. Their food, homes, and habits.

3. BIRDS AROUND US
Learn about how birds fly, how they migrate, why birds build different kinds of nests, and how they feed and train their babies.

4. FLOWERS AND WHAT THEY ARE
Are you sure you know a flower when you see one? Learn about garden and wild flowers, how some flowers got their names, and how they are used for food and fragrance.

5. TREES AND HOW THEY GROW
The story of trees from seed to seed, how trees feed themselves, how leaves turn color. Find out what trees do for man—and who ate "woodburgers."

6. OUR EARTH, WHAT IT IS
Learn about the inside and outside of the earth, what causes volcanoes and earthquakes, how the oceans and mountains came to be.

7. ROCKS AND WHAT THEY TELL US
Find out how rocks tell the story of the earth, why we find fossils of sea animals on mountaintops, what rock paintings tell us about cave men.

8. RIVERS, WHAT THEY DO
Learn about how rivers form, how they cut through mountains, why early pioneer trails, railroads, and even modern roads follow rivers.

9. PHYSICS, ITS MARVELS AND MYSTERIES
Learn about why planes fly, how we see and hear, how to make electricity. Find out how magnetism works and why you can bounce a Ping-pong ball on water.

10. THE BIG BUILDERS
Learn about the "gismo," why the Mohawk Indians work on tall buildings, how skyscrapers, bridges, and dams are built.

The Whitman Learn About Books have been carefully prepared with the editorial assistance of specialists in many fields.

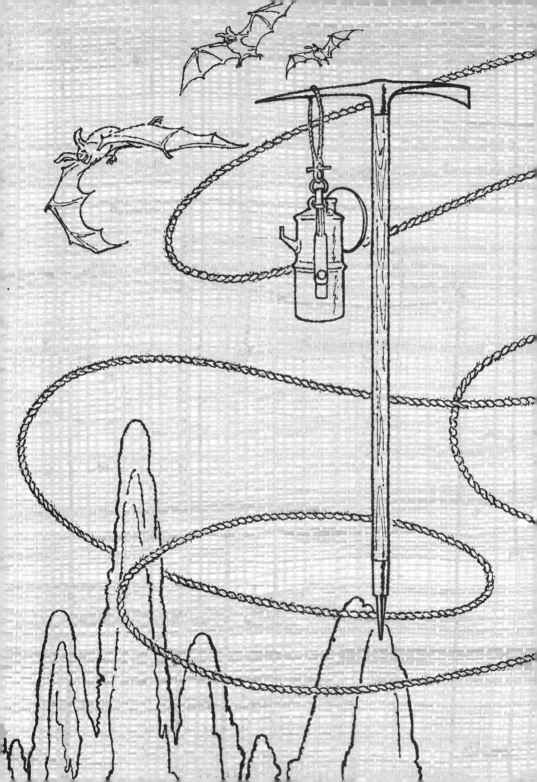